Mary, Bridget, & Noah Bly
February 1967

THE LITTLE LITURGY

A Children's
Introduction
to
Lutheran Worship

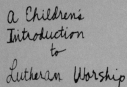

BY JAMES KERR

ILLUSTRATED
BY
Ollie Jensen

AUGSBURG PUBLISHING HOUSE
MINNEAPOLIS, MINN.

For nearly two thousand years Christians have gathered on Sunday mornings to praise God and to hear his Word. This meeting together is called the worship service. The worship service is almost the same each Sunday. The order or plan of worship is called the *liturgy*.

We use a liturgy, or plan of worship, so that we may all worship together, listening to or praising God, and asking forgiveness for our sins. Some parts of our Lutheran liturgy have been used by Christians for hundreds of years. Many of the words and much of the music in our Lutheran service are also used in other churches.

Long ago, before Jesus came to earth, God's people went to the synagogue on Saturday. This was called the *Sabbath*. Because Jesus rose again from the dead on Easter Sunday, Christians have made Sunday their day of worship. So every Lord's Day, or Sunday as we call it, is really a little Easter!

There are some parts of our plan of worship, or liturgy, that are different every Sunday. These are mainly the readings from the Bible, and a few of the prayers. The parts that change each Sunday are called *Propers*. The Propers teach us something different every Sunday. They are the same in many Christian churches around the world, and every Sunday millions of Christians throughout the world listen to the same Bible readings and pray the same prayers as we do in our church.

As we worship, we also learn. The worship service teaches us about our salvation in Jesus Christ. The *Sermon* and *Propers* teach us something special about Jesus' life, death, and resurrection. It is important that we listen to each part of the service, and it is important that we go to church each Sunday, because every service teaches us something new about Jesus.

SILENT SILENT SILENT

As we go into God's house we are quiet and thankful. The organ is playing a *Prelude* as we enter. *Prelude* means "to come before something important." The music helps to remind us how important our worship is to God.

The altar helper, called an *acolyte*, enters and lights the candles. The candlelights remind us that Jesus is the light of the world, and the altar reminds us of the great sacrifice of Jesus.

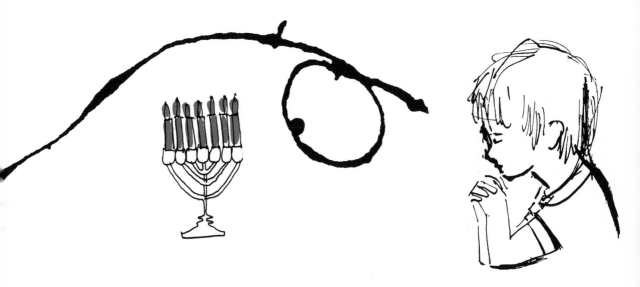

We bow our heads and ask Jesus to open our hearts to his love and his Word. We pray for our friends. We pray for the pastor who will bring us God's Word. Remember, we are with Jesus!

We are sometimes tempted to speak or whisper to those near us in church. But we should not disturb others. They are also talking to God and listening to his promises.

Worshiping is much more than going to church. To worship is to honor and praise God, and to let him know how much we love him and how much we look to him.

Now the pastor enters. He usually wears a white *surplice* over a black robe, called a *cassock*. Black is the color of sin and death. The pastor wears white, the color of the truth of the Gospel, over the black to tell us that the love of Jesus covers our sins. The pastor also wears a colored scarf around his neck. It is called a *stole*. This symbol tells us that the pastor is one who serves the people and who serves God. It is a different color for each season of the church year.

In the worship service the pastor will pray at the *altar* to God. He will speak to us from the *pulpit*. He will speak *for* us to God, and speak *to* us from God.

MAKE A JOYFUL NOISE UNTO THE LORD

We are ready to begin our worship service. This is the "preparing" part of the liturgy. The choir enters singing a hymn. We love to worship God by singing, and we remember David's words, "Make a joyful noise to the Lord." We join with the choir in singing the hymn.

This hymn is usually the *Processional,* or marching hymn.

IN THE NAME OF THE FATHER SON AND HOLY GHOST AMEN

Invocation

Now the pastor begins the service with these words:

In the Name of the Father, and of the Son, and of the Holy Ghost. This is called the *Invocation*. Invocation means calling upon God.

We answer:

AMEN.

When we answer Amen we are really saying, "This shall be so!"

We are saying that we have come to worship in the name of God. We worship God the Father who made us; God the Son who died and rose again for us; and God the Holy Ghost, who helps us know and do the things that Jesus would want us to do.

TO WORSHIP IS TO TAKE PART

We must remember that we have come to worship God, not to sit and watch others. To worship is to take part. No one else can worship for us. We are not worshiping when we sit and mumble and repeat words. We came to talk to God, and he is listening to us.

CONFESSION AND FORGIVENESS

Before God speaks to us, we prepare to hear his Word. We prepare by confessing our sins and asking forgiveness. To confess our sins to God is to tell God that we are sorry for the wrong thoughts that we have had and the wrong things that we have done.

Confession of Sins

The Confession of Sins

The pastor invites us to confess our sins:

Beloved in the Lord! Let us draw near with a true heart, and confess our sins unto God our Father, beseeching him, in the Name of our Lord Jesus Christ, to grant us forgiveness.

Then the pastor reminds us:

Our help is in the Name of the Lord.

We know that Jesus has helped us in many ways. We know that he made the whole earth for us and our fellowmen. We know that he watches over us. We know how great his name is, so we answer:

Who made heaven and earth.

who made heaven and earth

I SAID I WILL CONFESS MY TRANSGRESSIONS UNTO THE LORD

Once again the pastor asks us to confess our sins:

I said, I will confess my transgressions unto the Lord.

And we remember that for the sake of Jesus who died for us God has forgiven us. We know that he forgives us and loves us even more than our own parents do.

AND THOU FORGAVEST THE INIQUITY OF MY SIN

We remember his loving forgiveness by thanking him:

And thou forgavest the iniquity of my sin.

The service is really a *dialogue*, that is two people speaking to each other. We speak to God through the words in the *liturgy* and God speaks to us through the pastor.

The pastor turns to the *altar* to pray. He turns to the *altar* when he is speaking to God for us. We pray along with the pastor in our hearts:

Almighty God, our Maker and Redeemer, we poor sinners confess unto thee that we are by nature sinful and unclean, and that we have sinned against thee by thought, word, and deed. Wherefore we flee for refuge to thine infinite mercy, seeking and imploring thy grace, for the sake of our Lord Jesus Christ.

O MOST MERCIFUL GOD

Now we join the pastor in asking God to forgive our sins. We pray that we may know God better, we pray for strength to live as God wants us to live. The congregation prays together in the same words:

O most merciful God, who hast given thine only-begotten Son to die for us, have mercy upon us, and for his sake grant us remission of all our sins; and by thy Holy Spirit increase in us true knowledge of thee and of thy will, and true obedience to thy Word, that by thy grace we may come to everlasting life; through Jesus Christ our Lord. Amen.

Now God answers. God always answers prayer. We must remember that only he knows what is best for us. God speaks to us through our pastor. The pastor announces God's promise of forgiveness. He reminds us that God hears and forgives those who confess their sin and believe in Jesus:

Almighty God, our heavenly Father, hath had mercy upon us, and hath given his only Son to die for us, and for his sake forgiveth us all our sins. To them that believe on his Name he giveth power to become the sons of God, and bestoweth upon them his Holy Spirit. He that believeth, and is baptized, shall be saved. Grant this, O Lord, unto us all.

We know that God keeps his promises. We are happy that he forgives us and loves us. We answer God's promise of loving forgiveness by singing or saying:

Amen! (This shall be so!)

GLORY TO GOD

Introit

Until now we have been preparing ourselves for worship. Now we are ready to enter the main part of the service. The *Introit* is the next part. It means "entrance." The *Introits* are taken from the Psalms of the Old Testament. The *Introit* is the first *Proper,* or changeable part, of the service. It is read by the pastor or sung by the choir.

Gloria Patri

Now the main worship service has begun. Our first act of worship in this part of the service is the *Gloria Patri.* This means "Glory to God." Isn't this a beautiful worship hymn? This is the way we should begin every day, with a worshipful heart and willing hands.

GLORY BE TO THE FATHER AND TO THE SON AND TO THE HOLY GHOST

Glory be to the Father, and to the Son, and to the Holy Ghost: as it was in the beginning, is now, and ever shall be, world without end. Amen.

The next part of the service is called the *Kyrie*. The *Kyrie* may be the oldest part of our liturgy. Before congregations had books or written services, they often answered the pastor by saying, *"Kyrie eleison."* These words are from the Greek language and mean "Lord, have mercy." The use of the *Kyrie* began very early in the Christian church, and we continue to worship God as people have done for many centuries.

The *Kyrie,* as we call it today, is a prayer for grace and help.

Pastor: In peace let us pray to the Lord.

Response: Lord, have mercy.

Pastor: For the peace that is from above, and for the salvation of our souls, let us pray to the Lord.

Response: Lord, have mercy.

Pastor: For the peace of the whole world, for the well-being of the churches of God, and for the unity of all, let us pray to the Lord.

Response: Lord, have mercy.

Pastor: For this holy house, and for them that in faith, piety, and fear of God offer here their worship and praise, let us pray to the Lord.

KYRIE ELEISON ◦ KYRIE ELEISON◦

Response: Lord, have mercy.

Pastor: Help, save, pity, and defend us, O God, by thy grace.

Response: Amen.

Sometimes we use the shorter form of the *Kyrie:*

Pastor: Lord, have mercy upon us.

Response: Lord, have mercy upon us.

Pastor: Christ, have mercy upon us.

Response: Christ, have mercy upon us.

Pastor: Lord, have mercy upon us.

Response: Lord, have mercy upon us.

LORD HAVE MERCY, LORD HAVE MERCY,

Gloria in Excelsis

Now we are going to look back to Bethlehem. We join in the angels' Christmas song. The *Gloria in Excelsis,* which means "Glory in the Highest," is taken from Luke 2:14. This is one of the oldest hymns of the church. It is a hymn of joy and praise. It reminds us of the life of Jesus, beginning at Bethlehem, and of how God has had mercy upon us through his Son Jesus. It tells of Jesus, our Savior, who takes away our sin, and ends by praising him who sits at the right hand of God.

Pastor: Glory be to God on high!

Response: And on earth peace, good will toward men. We praise thee, we bless thee, we worship thee, we glorify thee, we give thanks to thee for thy great glory, O Lord God, heavenly King, God the Father Almighty.

O Lord, the only-begotten Son, Jesus Christ; O Lord God, Lamb of God, Son of the Father, that takest away the sin of the world, have mercy upon us. Thou that takest away the sin of the world, receive our prayer. Thou that sittest at the right hand of God the Father, have mercy upon us.

For thou only art holy; thou only art the Lord; thou only, O Christ, with the Holy Ghost, art most high in the glory of God the Father. Amen.

GLORIA

THE LORD BE WITH YOU

AND WITH THY SPIRIT

The Collect

The pastor turns to the congregation with a greeting called the *Salutation.*

The pastor says: The Lord be with you!

Response: And with thy spirit!

The first Christians had a beautiful way of greeting each other when they met. The first person would say this blessing, "The Lord be with you," and the other person answered, "And with thy spirit." This means a lot more than "Hello, how are you?" and the answer, "I'm fine, how are you?" The *Salutation* is used today as the pastor's prayer for his people, and the congregation's prayer for the pastor.

Once again the pastor invites us to prayer:

Let us pray.

LET US PRAY

The pastor turns to the *altar* since he is going to pray our prayer to God. In this prayer we are making final preparation to hear God's Word for our lives. This prayer is called the *Collect*, because it is a "collection" of our needs. It is a short prayer, one sentence in length, and is different each Sunday.

After the *Collect* we answer once more:
Amen!

THE OLD TESTAMENT LESSON AND THE EPISTLE

We have been preparing to hear God's Word. We have confessed our sins. We have heard God's answer that he forgives us. We have sung a hymn of praise and thanksgiving with the angels' song. We prayed for open hearts to hear God's marvelous Word.

The Old Testament Lesson
Here the pastor may read a Lesson from the Old Testament.

The Epistle
Now we come to the *Epistle*. Epistle means "letter." It is a reading from one of the "letters" of the apostles.

After hearing God's Word we joyfully answer:

Alleluia, Alleluia, Alleluia.

During Lent we sing instead:

Christ hath humbled himself, and become obedient unto death: even the death of the Cross.

ALLELUIA ALLELUIA ALLELUIA

THE GOSPEL

The Gospel

The next reading from God's Word is the *Gospel*. The *Gospel* reading will be from one of the four Gospels: Matthew, Mark, Luke, or John. To prepare for hearing the *Gospel* in some churches, the choir sings the *Gradual*. *Gradual* means "step." It leads from the *Epistle* to the *Gospel*.

In some churches, the pastor will use, instead of the *Gradual*, a special sentence for the season in the church year. This sentence is usually taken from the Psalms.

When the pastor announces the *Gospel* for the day, we praise God for his wonderful Word by singing:

Glory be to thee, O Lord.

We love and respect the Word of God. To show this, we stand while the *Gospel* is read to us. The *Gospel* for the day will tell us of some part of Christ's life here on earth. It will tell of his majesty, his humanity, his teaching, his power, or his love.

The pastor reads the *Gospel* to us.

Then we sing praise to God for his Word:

Praise be to thee, O Christ.

We are giving thanks for the privilege of hearing God's Word.

PRAISE BE TO THEE O CHRIST

The Creed

We came to church to worship God and to hear his Word. We came to be with other Christians and also to renew our faith. As a congregation we worship the same Savior. Now we have a chance to speak out about our faith. It is good to know that we all share this faith. The *Creed* (which means "I believe") reminds us that we are not alone. We know that we can enjoy being with other Christians who share our faith. As we confess our faith we also pledge our loyalty to God. We speak to our neighbor about our faith by saying, "This is what we believe!"

THE CREED

I believe in God the Father Almighty, Maker of heaven and earth:
And in Jesus Christ his only Son our Lord, Who was conceived by
the Holy Ghost, Born of the Virgin Mary, Suffered under Pontius
Pilate, Was crucified, dead, and buried: He descended into hell;
The third day he rose again from the dead; He ascended into heav-
en, And sitteth on the right hand of God the Father Almighty; From
thence he shall come to judge the quick and the dead.

I believe in the Holy Ghost; The Holy Christian Church, the
Communion of Saints; The Forgiveness of sins; The Resurrection
of the body, And the Life everlasting. Amen.

If there is to be a Baptism, turn to page 48 of this book. You
can follow the words if you look them up in your church hymnal.

The Hymn

Our church has often been called the singing church. Praising God with music and song is another way of worshiping. We join our voices together in worship as we sing the hymn before the sermon.

The Sermon

The *Sermon* is the part of the service where the pastor explains God's Word to us. He shows us what God's Word means in our lives. He tells us how we can know God better. The *Sermon* is also an invitation to accept Jesus.

The church has had many "preachers." The prophets of the Old Testament times preached God's Word to the people. John the Baptist was a preacher who prepared the people for the coming of Christ. Our pastor helps to prepare us for meeting Jesus, too.

At the end of the *Sermon* the pastor announces a blessing, called the *Votum:*

The Peace of God, which passeth all understanding, keep your hearts and minds through Christ Jesus.

We answer by singing or saying:

Amen! (This shall be so!)

The pastor is announcing God's promise of peace to all who love the Lord and worship him. It is a reminder that Jesus is with us wherever we go throughout the following week.

The Anthem

Once more we worship God in a different way. In many churches the choir sings an *Anthem.* The choir *Anthem,* or song, tells us about God, and it also is a special hymn of praise to God.

The Offering

Our *Offering* to God is an act of worship. It is not a "collection," but a way of giving praise. It is a way of showing our love to God for his many gifts to us. We cannot buy anything from God. We cannot ever pay him for what he has done for us. But we can offer him three things: our gifts, our life, and our prayers.

In offering ourselves, we sing the words of Psalm 51 in the *Offertory:*

Create in me a clean heart, O God: and renew a right spirit within me.

Cast me not away from thy presence: and take not thy Holy Spirit from me.

Restore unto me the joy of thy salvation: and uphold me with thy free Spirit.

CREATE
IN ME
A CLEAN
HEART
O
GOD

The Prayer of the Church

This prayer is said by the pastor for the congregation. This is part of our offering to God. We are offering God our praise, our intercession, and our life in his service. It is also a prayer of thanks, thanks for his work, his church, and his love.

This prayer has many parts. Different parts of the prayer are used on different Sundays. The following parts are used in many churches every Sunday. Sometimes more parts are added.

PRAYER

Pastor: Almighty God, the Father of our Lord Jesus Christ: We give thee praise and hearty thanks for all thy goodness and tender mercies. We bless thee for the love which hath created and doth sustain us from day to day. We praise thee for the gift of thy Son, our Saviour, through whom thou hast made known thy will and grace. We thank thee for the Holy Ghost, the Comforter; for thy holy Church, for the Means of Grace, for the lives of all faithful and godly men, and for the hope of the life to come. Help us to treasure in our hearts all that our Lord hath done for us; and enable us to show our thankfulness by lives that are given wholly to thy service;

Response: We beseech thee to hear us, good Lord.

Pastor: Save and defend thy Church Universal, purchased with the precious Blood of Christ. Give it pastors and ministers according to thy Spirit, and strengthen it through the Word and the holy Sacraments. Make it perfect in love and in all good works, and establish it in the faith delivered to the saints. Sanctify and unite thy people in all the world, that one holy Church may bear witness to thee, the God and Father of all;

Response: We beseech thee to hear us, good Lord.

SEND FORTH THY LIGHT AND THY TRUTH

Pastor: Send forth thy light and thy truth into all the earth, O Lord. Raise up, we pray thee, faithful servants of Christ to labor in the Gospel at home and in distant lands;

Response: We beseech thee to hear us, good Lord.

Pastor: Preserve our Nation in righteousness and honor, and continue thy blessings to us as a people, that we may lead a quiet and peaceable life, in all godliness and honesty. Grant health and favor to all who bear office in our land (especially to the President and the Congress, the Governor and Legislature of this State), and help them to acknowledge and obey thy holy will;

Response: We beseech thee to hear us, good Lord.

Pastor: God of mercies, we pray thee to comfort with the grace of thy Holy Spirit all who are in sorrow or need, sickness or adversity. Remember those who suffer persecution for the faith. Have mercy upon those to whom death

draws near. Bring consolation to those in sorrow or mourning. And to all grant a measure of thy love, taking them into thy tender care;

Response: We beseech thee to hear us, good Lord.

Pastor: We remember with thanksgiving those who have loved and served thee in thy Church on earth, who now rest from their labors (especially those most dear to us, whom we name in our hearts before thee). Keep us in fellowship with all thy saints, and bring us at length to the joy of thy heavenly kingdom;

Response: We beseech thee to hear us, good Lord.

Pastor: All these things, and whatever else thou seest that we need, grant us, O Father, for his sake who died and rose again, and now liveth and reigneth with thee in the unity of the Holy Ghost, one God, world without end.

Response: Amen.

HOLY COMMUNION

When God's family takes part in the Lord's Supper in Holy Communion, the complete liturgy is used. If there is to be no Communion, turn to page 42.

The Communion

The communion service is called *The Thanksgiving*. You will want to follow the words used in this part of the service as you find them in your hymnal.

The *Preface* introduces the communion service. This is a changeable part of the service, and it will be different in every part of the church year.

The pastor and congregation sings or says:

Pastor: The Lord be with you.

Response: And with thy spirit.

Pastor: Lift up your hearts.

Response: We lift them up unto the Lord.

Pastor: Let us give thanks unto the Lord our God.

Response: It is meet and right so to do.

The pastor turns to the altar as he sings or says: It is truly meet, right, and salutary, that we should at all times, and in all places, give thanks unto thee, O Lord, Holy Father, Almighty, Everlasting God.

Therefore with Angels and Archangels, and with all the company of heaven, we laud and magnify thy glorious Name; evermore praising thee, and saying:

SANCTUS

Then we sing the *Sanctus,* a song that is much like the *Gloria in Excelsis.* This is a song of praise based on the words the crowds sang to Jesus on Palm Sunday.

THE SANCTUS

Holy, holy, holy, Lord God of Sabaoth; Heaven and earth are full of thy glory; Hosanna in the highest.

Blessed is he that cometh in the Name of the Lord; Hosanna in the highest.

WORDS OF INSTITUTION

The *Words of Institution* are the words of Jesus when he gave the disciples the Last Supper. The pastor reads these words at the altar:

Sometimes the pastor uses the *Prayer of Thanksgiving,* which contains the Words of Institution.

AGNUS DEI

Next we sing the *Agnus Dei,* which means "Lamb of God." The words were spoken by John the Baptist when he announced the arrival of Jesus.

THE WORDS OF INSTITUTION

Our Lord Jesus Christ, in the night in which he was betrayed, took bread; and, when he had given thanks, he brake it and gave it to his disciples, saying, Take, eat; this is my Body, which is given for you; this do in remembrance of me.

After the same manner also, he took the cup, when he had supped, and, when he had given thanks, he gave it to them, saying, Drink ye all of it; this cup is the New Testament in my Blood, which is shed for you, and for many, for the remission of sins; this do, as oft as ye drink it, in remembrance of me.

Next we pray the *Lord's Prayer.*

Pastor: The peace of the Lord be with you alway.

Response: And with thy spirit.

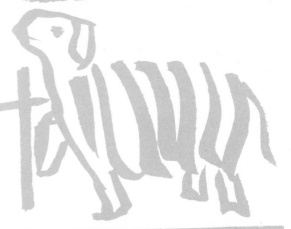

AGNUS DEI

O Christ, thou Lamb of God, that takest away the sin of the world, have mercy upon us.

O Christ, thou Lamb of God, that takest away the sin of the world, have mercy upon us.

O Christ, thou Lamb of God, that takest away the sin of the world, grant us thy peace. Amen.

When the members of the congregation receive Jesus Christ in the bread and wine, it is a very important and happy occasion.

THE POST-COMMUNION

Then the congregation sings or says:

Lord, now lettest thou thy servant depart in peace: according to thy word;

For mine eyes have seen thy salvation: which thou hast prepared before the face of all people;

A light to lighten the Gentiles: and the glory of thy people Israel.

Glory be to the Father, and to the Son, and to the Holy Ghost:

As it was in the beginning, is now, and ever shall be, world without end. Amen.

After the Holy Communion the pastor offers a prayer of thanksgiving and pronounces the *Benediction.*

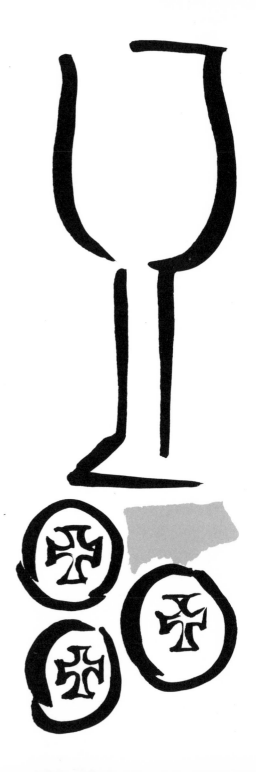

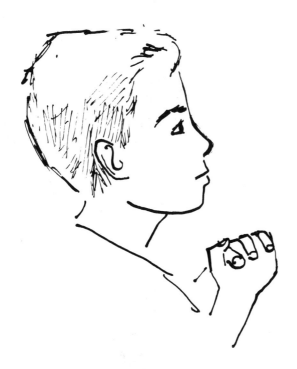

The Lord's Prayer

"Teach us to pray," the disciples asked Jesus. Then Jesus said, "Pray in these words," and the prayer he taught them is called the *Lord's Prayer:*

Our Father, who art in heaven, Hallowed be thy Name, Thy kingdom come, Thy will be done, on earth as it is in heaven. Give us this day our daily bread; And forgive us our trespasses, as we forgive those who trespass against us; And lead us not into temptation, But deliver us from evil. For thine is the kingdom, and the power, and the glory, for ever and ever. Amen.

This is the prayer of the children of God. Hundreds of years ago, in the early church, only the believers were allowed to learn this prayer. It was a secret guarded very jealously. And it was taught to a new member only when the congregation was certain that the new member really loved the Word of God.

Our Father Who art in heaven Hallowed be thy name

BENEDICTION

The *Benediction* is a blessing which the pastor announces to us:

The Lord bless thee, and keep thee. The Lord make his face shine upon thee, and be gracious unto thee. The Lord lift up his countenance upon thee, and give thee peace: In the Name of the Father, and of the Son, and of the Holy Ghost.

How wonderful to know that I begin the new week taking with me God's blessing! For this is not a prayer that I may have God's blessing, but an announcement of God's promise to be with me always! Joyfully, I answer:

Amen, Amen, Amen!

Jesus has promised that where two or three are gathered in his name, there he would be also. As we began the service in his name, we know that he has been with us. And through his Word and promises we know that we have been with him.

Our worship service is over, but our worship of God should never stop. The service in the church must have a time to begin and a time to end. But our lives should be one long worship service to God. To live and think and do as God would want us to, this is a worshipful life.

As we leave the church again we hear the organ play. This is the *Postlude,* which means "to come after." Listen and hear how joyful and victorious the music is! This is to help us remember the joy and victory of the Christian life.

THE BAPTISMAL SERVICE

Very often during a service a small child will be baptized. When a child is baptized, a special part of the liturgy is used. This is called the *Order for the Baptism of Infants.*

Baptism is a Sacrament, a "special act of God." When you were very small, your parents brought you to church to be baptized. This meant that God was accepting you into his family. At the time of your Baptism, your parents spoke for you. When you are old enough you will be confirmed. In the confirmation service you will make your own confession of faith in God.

Our baptismal day is an important one. It is really a kind of birthday. It is the birthday of our entering into the family of God.